Inbound Marketing For Startups Without All The Hassles

Content Market Business Growth Strategies To Skyrocket Your Sales

© Copyright 2017 by Boris Vanderwall - All rights reserved.

This document is geared towards providing exact and reliable information in regards to the topic and issue covered. The publication is sold with the idea that the publisher is not required to render accounting, officially permitted, or otherwise, qualified services. If advice is necessary, legal or professional, a practiced individual in the profession should be ordered.

- From a Declaration of Principles which was accepted and approved equally by a Committee of the American Bar Association and a Committee of Publishers and Associations.

In no way is it legal to reproduce, duplicate, or transmit any part of this document in either electronic means or in printed format. Recording of this publication is strictly prohibited and any storage of this document is not allowed unless with written permission from the publisher. All rights reserved.

The information provided herein is stated to be truthful and consistent, in that any liability, in terms of inattention or otherwise, by any usage or abuse of any policies, processes, or directions contained within is the solitary and utter responsibility of the recipient reader. Under no circumstances will any legal responsibility or blame be held against the publisher for any reparation, damages, or monetary loss due to the information herein, either directly or indirectly.

Respective authors own all copyrights not held by the publisher.

The information herein is offered for informational purposes solely, and is universal as so. The presentation of the information is without contract or any type of guarantee assurance.

The trademarks that are used are without any consent, and the publication of the trademark is without permission or backing by the trademark owner. All trademarks and brands within this book are for clarifying purposes only and are the owned by the owners themselves, not affiliated with this document.

Table Of Contents

Introduction 7
Chapter One: A Quick Look at Inbound Marketing 9
   How Does Inbound Marketing Work? 11
   Inbound Marketing vs. Outbound Marketing 21
   The Benefits of Inbound Marketing 23
   Tips for Inbound Marketing 29
   "The Inbound Methodology" 31
      What is the Inbound Marketing Methodology? 32
Chapter Two: Local Inbound Marketing 38
   The Four Pillars of Marketing 40
      Building Relationships with the Contact you Already Have 41
      Attracting New Clients 44
      Get Your Name Out There! 47
      Creating Effective Communication 49
   Benefits of Local Inbound Marketing 51
   Tips for Local Inbound Marketing 55
Chapter Three: Content Marketing 59
   Content Marketing vs. Inbound Marketing 59
      Inbound Marketing 62
      Content Marketing 63
      The Core Differences 64
   Benefits of Content Marketing 68
   How to Create a Content Marketing Strategy 73
      What is your goal? 73
      Find Out Your Target Audience 76
      Run an Audit 78
      Manage Your Content 79

Chapter Four: What Kind of Content is there to Publish? 81
   Forms of Content 81
      Blogs 81
      Webinars 82
      Surveys 84
      Memes 85
      User Generated Content 86
      Pictures 87
   Tips for Online Content Publishing 88
Chapter Five: Business to Business (B2B) Inbound Marketing 99
   How to Use Social Media to Promote you B2B 102
   The B2B Funnel 107
   Tips and Tricks for B2B Inbound Marketing ..111
Chapter Six: What You Need to Know Before You Go 116
   Warnings and Advice 116
   Things You Need to Do 123
   Finances 127
Conclusion 129

Introduction

When you participate in marketing, the goal is to promote or advertise a product or idea, right? I'm sure that you also knew that there are different types of marketing, many of which have different strategies and ways to attract suitable buyers or investors.

If you didn't' know that, don't worry about it because, in the next few chapters, we are going to have an in-depth discussion about marketing, the different kind of marketing and the strategies that you can use in each on to expand your business and get you sale to skyrocket.

Chapter One: A Quick Look at Inbound Marketing

As we've already mentioned there are a few different types of marketing. The first kind of marketing we are going to talk about is inbound marketing. The official definition of inbound marketing is "the process of attracting the attention of prospects, via content creation, before they are even ready to buy" (thecenterforsalesstrategy.com). This type of marketing is said to be one of the best and most used ways to get customers to migrate to your business and is cost effective.

Before we can really begin, we should make sure that you understand the term "lead." When you are looking for leads, it simply means that you are looking for people to buy your product or business; you are looking for prospective consumers—people who are most likely and willing to buy a certain product. It is important to note that coming up with leads can be easy, but actually getting them to buy can become the problem. This is the whole point of inbound marketing. You want to use inbound marketing to actually attract the leads or "audiences" that you are trying to appeal to.

For example, if you are to be putting a new acne medication on the market, you may aim for your leads to be younger adults. However, once you put out surveys, advertise, test the products and actually get them out on the market, you may see that your product actually appeals more to teenagers. So, really, all along, your leads should have been more in the pre-teen/teenager age range.

You may see this used in real like for a product called Proactive. Proactive is a face wash that has been out on the market for years. When they first began advertising for the product, they showed commercials of young adults with clear skin. Then, when they realized who their real demographic was, they began using celebrity endorsement to attract the young fans of these celebrities. For instance, you may remember Justin Bieber being featured in these commercials, whose audience is mostly teenage girls.

So, how can we use inbound marketing to attract more leads? Well, that's where the strategies come in! In the next few pages, we are going to talk about what we can do to increase your sales and help get your business booming.

How Does Inbound Marketing Work?

When you dive into the idea of inbound marketing, you should have a good idea of what you are getting yourself into, right? Well, that would include knowing an outline of how this inbound marketing thing works and what you should do before you start. So let's get into it.

The first thing you'll want to do, after educating yourself on inbound marketing, is to assemble a team to help you carry out all the duties and odd jobs that come with this marketing type. A good idea is to describe to them—really help them understand—exactly what marketing entails if they do not already know, and that inbound marketing is a "go-all-in" strategy.

This means that you may run into problems with customers, finances, and much more.

So who exactly should you have on your team? Some people that you should makes sure are present include marketing strategists, content copywriters, web developers and marketing coordinators. You may be asking why you need all these people. Well it may help to know exactly what they do so that you may understand why you need them.

A marketing strategist has the job of organizing and designing marketing campaigns as well as coming up with different ways that your company can get buyers. They will be the ones that will come to you for ideas for attracting customers. They will also be assigned with communicating with the customers, as they spread the word about business through one or multiple strategies and media. Even though this is something that everyone should strive for, the marketing strategist's main concern should be customer satisfaction. Recommending ideas and giving advice is something that you should be able to get out of these co-workers as well! They should have a good hold on the marketing business and should be able to help you choose between certain strategies.

A content copywriter, on the other hand, would be handed the task of writing out any blogs, posts, and other content about the product in order to promote it. A good example of this would be a company owning a Facebook account. A copywriter would do the job of posting new ideas, items and merchandise in order to attract customers. You may even feel that—if your copywriters have a lot to do and a lot of work on their plate—a copy editor to look over your writer's work is a good idea as well. These people would work together to keep an eye on promotional posts and to write up and proofread a lot of the things that you will be putting online or out in public.

You need to remember that today's society is very social media and Internet based. Since you probably already know that yourself, you'll agree when we suggest having your own company or product website. Here you should have information on your company, the products you sell, the ideas you have for the future, and maybe even a place for your customers to buy products and such. However, if you have your own website, it is strongly advised that you have a web developer or web designer. This person can help you design a beautiful and smooth website that is easy to navigate for both experienced workers and brand new customers. Your web developers are also the people you should be able to go to when you think you have a problem with your website or if it is not working as good as it should.

Finally, there is one more type of person that you should consider to have on your team: marketing coordinators. A marketing coordinator is very similar to a marketing strategist, they may be able to work together to for the ultimate marketing specialist to help you with collecting and analyzing sales data and success statistics as well as "keeping promotional materials ready" (hiring.monster.com).

So, as you can see, these different people all have some sort of important job to take care of. And trying to do this all by yourself would be crazy. You would probably become overwhelmed and resent your job fairly quickly and no one wants that! With all the opportunities the world has to offer you in this day in age, it would be crazy not to invest a little bit of time, effort and money into finding the right people to help you with your ideas, dreams, and ambitions.

"What else comes with inbound marketing?"

Before making the change to inbound marketing, you want to assess your current statistics and data. You should do this before you invest in any new marketing programs. Making sure that you have all of your business in order is much more important than you think. There are a few questions that you should ask yourself as well, the most important being "What is our current financial situation?" This is very important, because inbound marketing is an investment, meaning that you have to "spend money to make money" as the saying goes. You should also have a good idea of what your current marketing assets are and how they are working. If you are successful, you may want to bring some of those assets along with you when you make the change to inbound marketing.

For example, if you find that advertising and promoting your business, services, and or products on the Internet via social media is bringing in leads and customers then it may be a good idea to continue doing it even when you have made the switch to inbound marketing.

You'll also want to "define your marketing goals" (blog.hubspot.com). Going into any marketing strategy blindly is always a bad idea; you should have a plan, know what services or products you want to sell, and why you want to sell them. You should also have a good idea of where you want to go to with your company. Actually, you are you are advised to make—and keep in mind—some goals that you want to achieve in a set amount of time. You should ask yourself questions such as "What are we trying to achieve?" and "What does your business want people to do?" (blog.hubspot.com).You can use those questions and the acronym "SMART" to come up with efficient and entirely possible goals.

But what is SMART? Smart stands for specific, measurable, attainable, realistic and timely. You should be very specific with your goals, meaning you should know exactly what you want and you should make it very clear to the people working for you in your company. You should also make sure that you can measure your success. This could mean having records to look back on to assess your progress. The goal you set should also be achievable and realistic. They should not be too far fetched and you should be able to see them achieved in the near future; you should be able to imagine yourself where you would be at the end of that goal. Finally, you should also see to it that your goal is timely. It should not take forever to achieve your goal. With the SMART acronym, you can sit down, plan your goals, and—in time—achieve them!

This may be one of the most important things that you want to do before you begin participating in inbound marketing: define your demographic. Finding your key demographic should one of the first things that happen when you decide to promote an idea, service, or product. Defining the target audience will help you with finding the best marketing strategy, as well. For example, if you are trying to develop a product that targets people in the age range of 15 to 25, you should try your best to aim for strategies that would reach those leads effectively. You could do this by using social media, a blog, or other Internet sources. On the opposite side of the spectrum, you could put out information that would affect an older population for a certain product.

You may want to think about developing a plan that you can refer back to throughout your marketing journey. This will include gathering up all the things that we have talked about in the past few pages and organizing it in any sort of table or organized format. If you have this, then you can look at it throughout the process and assess where you are, where you should be, and whether or not you are getting where you want to be; which is closer to your goals.

So, what kind of questions should you ask yourself in order to produce your business plan? Well, other than what we have already talked about here, you should think about the technology that you may need. Despite your demographic, you have to think about the fact that inbound marketing is all about using technology to share information. The information will be used to peak the interest and gain the trust of buyers. So you need to determine all the software and services that you are going to need in order to achieve all that you want to.

After you've done all of this, you can finally begin! The first thing you want to do is build a website. This is where your business plan and your web designer and developers will come in! With the help of the people you've hired and decide to work beside, you can get a website built that is easy to navigate and can provide information for anyone who wants to know more about your services. When it comes to your website, you'll want to make sure that you include things like a search engine, accessible to mobile users, which can be used on as many browsers as possible, and actual content. That means blogs, comment sections, forums, and the like.

Now that you have your website up in running order, you'll want to give your copywriters and editors a call. It's time to get some content onto your website and make sure that you can gain the attention of potential buyers. You could ask people to try and review your products and even to write blogs on your website. It is recommended that you post "at least twice a week for the first three months" (blog.hubspot.com) in order to gain more readers and then you can taper off a little toward maybe once a week. Using different social media is another great way to find clients. Once you have accounts and emails open for each branch of your company, you can connect an account or email to social media including Instagram, Twitter, Facebook and Tumblr. You may also be able to find opportunities outside of your company's website. This can include books, e-books, and videos along with guest blogging, webinars, and even vlogging (video blogging).

With all of this information, along with what we are going to talk about in more detail within the next few chapters, your sales will not be stalled for very much longer.

Inbound Marketing vs. Outbound Marketing

Before we talk about the benefits of inbound marketing, we are going to talk about the complete opposite of inbound marketing: outbound marketing. Outbound marketing is the older, more hated (by potential buyers and most start ups), and more time-consuming. In the attempt to direct you away from outbound marketing at any cost, we're going to look at why inbound marketing is worlds better than outbound marketing.

With the older outbound marketing, it seemed that communication was a "one-way street" meaning that the seller sends the buyer text messages, email, and even gives them phone calls in some cases. Often times, the potential customer sees this as pushing products or services on customers. This usually results in customers losing their patience, getting annoyed and unsubscribing from phone calls and newsletters. Not only do they unsubscribe, but this usually keeps them from subscribing or paying attention to your newsletter and other business, as well. In fact, 91% of all email users that were subscribed to company emails have unsubscribed at some point in time and 44% of the emails that they received were never even opened.

We can contrast that with inbound marketing where the advertisements are not pushed into buying anything; they come to you! Unlike outbound marketing, you won't even need to send out emails or newsletters. With the help of different strategies like using different social media, you will catch the attention of prospective customers. Not only do marketers and companies enjoy this type of marketing due to its low cost and time efficiency, but potential customers prefer it due to the less "annoying" nature of it. There is no badgering or constant messaging, emailing, or phoning in order to get a customer's attention. It's sad, actually, that outbound marketing is used so much, as about 84% of 25 to 34-year-olds have stopped going to their favorite websites due to the constant "intrusive or irrelevant advertising" (blog.hubspot.com).

The Benefits of Inbound Marketing

The Internet was invented by not one person, but many different people. It started off as something called the ARPANET used as a weapon of sorts during the cold war. It was proposed as a "galactic network" in order for people with computers hooked up to it to communicate and send messages to each other. This was in 1962. Then it began to grow. Researchers and scientist figured out a way to send files from one computer to another in the 1980s and in 1991, a man named Tim Berners-Lee created the "World Wide Web": a place where people could communicate not just through files, but a place where anyone that was connected to that web could talk to each other in some way.

Ever since then, people have been using the Internet as a way to communicate, get news out there, and yes, promote businesses. And this is why the Internet is so important to inbound marketers. They are able to sit in the comfort of their own home and promote their business. And that is the biggest advantage that you have when it comes to inbound marketing: the Internet. Anyone with a computer, an Internet connection, and an idea can promote their business and make money—no matter how small their business may be.

In one day, there is a recorded over five billion Google searches daily and that is why having your business, products and ideas attached to keywords (words that bring up results in an Internet search) is so important. Someone could be conducting a regular search of "marketing" or "business" or even "banana" if you wanted and they could find your business. However, using unrelated keywords isn't recommended, as it betrays another one of inbound marketing's greatest advantage: trust.

Trust from your clients is one of those things that should be important to any business provider. However, sometimes that is not the case. Something else that you may want to look to earn is respect, loyalty and credibility. These are all things that letting your customers come to you can earn you. Instead of badgering and harassing future customers, you can instead build a relationship with them, allowing them to come to you and make their own decisions. The type of annoyance that comes with outbound marketing, as stated before, is what makes people run away from businesses and makes them seem desperate, and can result in the decline of customers.

It's also been stated briefly here that inbound marketing is straight up just more affordable. "A study by Demand Metric showed that inbound marketing generates three times more leads than outbound marketing while costing 62 percent less" (quarizmi.com). This means that not only is inbound marketing one of the most effective marketing strategies, but it is also one of the cheapest (in comparison to outbound marketing). Right away, you could assume that inbound is more affordable than outbound anyway because of the simple fact that you don't have to hire people to send mail, emails, notifications, and phone calls. It is from this that we can conclude that inbound marketing is more efficient in terms of time as well.

With no emails to send to thousands of people and no phone calls to make to who knows how many more people, there is more time to use to put into content, designing of websites, collaborations with other companies, and improving customer service and products. This will help a boat-load when it comes to sales, hence it being another reason why using inbound marketing as your main strategy is one of the healthiest and best decisions that you can make as a business owner for you, your workers and your business.

Since inbound marketing is also a two-way street—connecting with your leads and potential customers—it helps build a healthy relationship with customers and you can use the extra time to see to those healthy relationships! Respond to personal emails, inquiries, and more; show your customers or people who show interest in your services respect and kindness and they will give you back the same as well as their business and their cooperation.

In a certain light, you can also say that this is all connected to simplifying the job and making it easier on yourself. This can not only have a positive impact on your business but on you as a business person and even your workers. When you are stressed and everything seems to overwhelm you—even the smallest things—you can end up crashing and burning before your product or services even go on the market. A good idea is to use inbound marketing as your way out of the stressful mess that sometimes business can turn into. The best thing that you can do it to make sure that your workers are happy and that they (and yourself) are not doing anything that cannot be handled.

Along with this, creating content can sometimes help you de-stress and allow for you to become more open and happy about your job. This is more targeted at your workers, but when your workers are stressed, your business does not operate correctly. It has actually been proven that the creativity and organization of a blog post can effectively reduce stress, taking your mind off many of the troubles that you could be facing throughout your day or week. Blogging daily can literally improve your performance and allow you to become a better writer and produce more quality content. This will help your business greatly, as more productive, happy workers is something that you will find to be much more pleasant than you'll ever know.

We already know that when you put out content in order to grab the attention of viewers, buyers and even investors, you are not only helping your business, but you are also adding "value to the world in terms of content and knowledge" (quarizmi.com). This helps create awareness for certain problems, issues, and/or troubles. Creating awareness and seeming less selfish will in turn get you the trust and acknowledgment that you need from many Internet communities, social media and even Internet celebrities that follow the same passions, hence gaining you and your business respect.

You'll also find that due to the smaller amount of work that you have to do, you'll have fewer workers. This means that you'll have the chance to get to know your workers and to have a better relationship with them. This encourages a positive work environment along with team spirit. Having happy workers, as said before, means a happy business.

Tips for Inbound Marketing

When you first start something, you'll want to have a few tips and tricks up your sleeve for when you run into a block and do not know what to do next. So, here are some of those tricks that you can use anytime you are in times of trouble.

One of the first things that you should do to is design a website that, not only has enjoyable, quality content, but you should also have a call-to-action on the very front page. This should be a large part of the view and is most likely going to be the focal point of the introductory page. This catches people's attention, causing them to click on any "Learn More" buttons (something else that you should make sure there are plenty of) so that they can get all the information they need to make the decision to invest in your services or not.

You may also want to consider using a "landing page" this is not necessarily a home page, but one that opens up right into the content. You'll want to makes sure that there are plenty of visuals, making the page appealing to the viewer. This will be attractive, making them click on more; if the web page is boring, then it is most likely that the person that clicked on your website in the first place will leave just as quickly as they came. And you will not be the only website doing this! About 56% of all websites open up to the landing page in order to attract readers, buyers, investors and even workers.

Many companies find that using quotes from past customers is great for finding new customers. It is proven that 88% of people trust the review of "real people" instead of the word of the company. This has actually caused an increase in marketing effectiveness of about 54%. If that's not incentive enough to try this method out, I don't know what is!

One of the most important things that you can do when inbound marketing is keep your research updated. You should keep on updating your research even after you think that you have searched the topic to what you think is completion. Things on the Internet change and if you have worked in business before, you'll know that new strategies and new information are put out there every day. So it is important that you keep in mind the idea of re-researching your stuff and taking new strategies into consideration.

"The Inbound Methodology"

For those of you who do not know, we use the word methodology to describe a series of methods that one can use to enhance a particular study or activity. Almost everything that you do can have a methodology, depending on what it is, who is carrying out the actions, and what you plan to do with it in the future. The easiest example that I can think of cooking.

When your mother use to cook you her famous banana bread, she probably had a number of methods that led to her bread being light and fluffy as well as sweet and delicious. This could include not beating the batter too hard, beating the eggs before adding them to the batter or using egg whites instead of whole eggs or even just cooking the batter at a certain temperature. All of these things—or methods—add together to give you a methodology. So, if you look at it, this whole selection would count as a methodology because of the combination of different things that you can do to increase sales and, intern, profits.

What is the Inbound Marketing Methodology?

The inbound marketing methodology can be broken up into five stages, content creation and distribution, lifecycle marketing, personalization, multichannel and integration.

These five stages can be use—in that order—to enhance sales and make sure that your business goes down in the books someday as successful as possible.

Let's look at the five stages a little more closely.

You already know that creating content is crucial for getting views, subscribers, followers, and, eventually, customers, but it also allows people to interact with your writers and managers. When you create content—writing blogs and uploading videos—you allow potential customers to learn exactly what your company is all about. You also give them a chance to interact with your workers by posting comments, sharing, and subscribing or following.

All of these things come together to create the perfect combination to attract people and potential customers to your site. This in turn allows you to make more money, up your sales, and so much more.

Now, what about the distribution part of creating content? This simply means the "putting out" or "sharing" of the content that you've created. That would include adding the content to a website or posting it on Youtube and Facebook.

Now you want to start marketing. This is the lifecycle marketing stage. It simply involves finding people that would like to try your product or services and asking them to give their opinion to people on the Internet. When you make it to this stage of marketing, you could contact people with a high amount of followers on some sort of social media such as Facebook, Instagram, Youtube, Twitter, or Tumblr. By doing this, your product will be heard of from many different social media stars and potential customers will get the chance to decide whether or not the product is worth their money.

For example, a company called Skinny Teatox offers different kinds of teas that do different things. To help spread the news of their business, they have a section on their website called "Free Tea." When you click on the link it brings you to a page that explains that they will send their product to any person with a blog with a large amount of readers or followers for free. They say that they want a completely honest review. They do this to makes sure that they have the respect of their future customers.

Asking people to do untruthful reviews can get you in trouble in terms of loss of business and complaints. Nobody wants to spend their money on something that is promised to work when it actually does not.

Next, you want to personalize your product or promotions. You can "tailor your content to the wants and needs of the people who are viewing it" (hubspot.com). For example, you may have a young, female demographic. Having blogs about makeup, hair and other beauty tips and such might be a good idea as it will attack a lot of that certain audience. This way they may not only find your blogs appealing, but they will also show a lot of interest in your product and invest in it. That means more sales and eventually better service.

Make sure that you choose the right demographic for the product that you are selling or vice versa. This could lead to the building or tearing down of your company or business. When you are aiming for the wrong demographic, no one will buy your product. For example, if you are trying to sell a tablet to people who don't know how to use tablets, then they are not going to buy it. A better demographic for a tablet or electronics would be students. Of course, not only students can buy your product, but your main promoters will be young people who are using technology daily to carry out their everyday tasks.

Once you gain regular customers or learn a thing or to about the people who are giving you their business, you will know what they look for in terms of sales and promotions. This will help you get a good hold on what you have to do to keep your current customers and, even more importantly, attract new ones.

Now, the multichannel stage is going to come almost automatically and naturally. The inbound marketing strategy is considered to be multichannel by nature due to the idea that you are going to the customer, inspiring the desire to be more interactive with you as a result. So there really isn't much to say about this stage.

Finally, the integration stage. The formal definition of integrating is to combine or put together steps to make one large "well-oiled machine". So now to put everything together would be the fifth and final stage called integration. Adding the content creation and distribution, personalization, marketing and the multichannel aspect of inbound marketing, you are simply integrating all the methods, creating a methodology.

Chapter Two: Local Inbound Marketing

So even though the basic premise of inbound marketing is to attract business by providing information and letting the customers come to you, there are different kinds of inbound marketing. We are going to talk about each one in depth but we can begin with local inbound marketing. This type of marketing is usually one that is used by local business owners. This can include a local Mary Brown's restaurant or even a local clothing boutique.

You may have the basic business Facebook or Twitter page, but this may not be enough. Making the move to create an "online presence" that will promote your local business and make your community aware of what your services offer to them. This could mean starting with flyers. It may not be the Internet use that you would think, but getting flyers out, around your community can help raise the awareness, getting people to check out your website and look for more information. Of course, this leads to phone calls, emails, and even visits from the locals to gather information or even ask questions.

So, what makes local inbound marketing different to the inbound marketing that we know so much about now? Well, when you practice local inbound marketing, you'll find that you're simply presenting your business to an audience who has shown interest in those particular products locally—in your home town or your neighborhood. In contrast with that, inbound marketing can be described as a world wide event; something that not only people in your hometown, but people all over the world can request your services.

Local inbound marketing isn't all about your hometown, city or neighborhood; it can also be described as practicing inbound market in a certain targeted geographical area. For example, you might want to find business in towns near mountains in order to get interest in your climbing gear. Or you may be a large company looking to get interest from other companies in order to buy your gondola business. There are very few things that separate local inbound marketing from inbound marketing, but you'll see that the biggest difference is the area. You "set up shop" closer to where you'd like to sell the product or services.

Of course, you are still advised, as stated above, to set up websites, create awareness, connect with potential customers on social media and much more, but you are also encouraged to make them aware of your location; especially when it comes to you seeking business with other companies. The fact that you are a local establishment will win you big points. This is because many businesses would rather an easier, more efficient contact so that business can run smoother.

The Four Pillars of Marketing

This is important to know for not only inbound marketing but local inbound marketing as well. You should educate yourself on "the four pillars of marketing." This can help you build a successful marketing strategy so that your business can pick up and you can get on your feet.

Building Relationships with the Contact you Already Have

There are things that you can do to build trust with the few contacts that you may already have. Make sure that your customers feel completely fulfilled by asking them to complete customer satisfaction surveys. This will show that you are willing to make changes that will cause the happiness and satisfaction that your future customers can look forward to. As you follow the advice of past clients, you can expect more customers to slowly flock to your company for your services. This will because you will slowly bring your company to a place where, not only you will feel accomplished and pleased with your business and the services that you provide, but your customers will feel completely satisfied when they leave your building or website.

You can also guarantee customer satisfaction by training your workers in such a way that they'll know how to deal with any questions, concerns or problems that may arise when dealing with customers. This is especially important that the customer service representatives are trained this way. Without this, they may not be able to completely help the client with certain problems.

Promoting groups is another way that you can hear feedback from clients that you may have. This can be done through Facebook, Instagram, and Twitter or even in real life. These groups can be somewhere that customers can voice their honest opinions. They can get a chance to talk to company and customer service representatives in an attempt to better the services that you are providing.

Something else that is extremely important is to make sure that you maintain communication with your clients. Communication is key. When you have good communication with the community what you've built will stay tight-knit and close. This means that you will know when your company will need any improving or adjustments in terms of client or customer service.

Tracking referrals—both incoming and outgoing—is something that your workers should get into as well. By tracking the incoming referrals, you can analyze the number of clients that are recommended to come to you by other companies or even other clients. Then there are the outgoing referrals. This would include you telling your customer or client that they could go somewhere else to get help or somewhere along those lines.

Assessing the number of outgoing referrals can help you understand a number of things. This could include noticing the number of people that you may not be able to help as well as someone else. You can analyze what you need to make those services that you have trouble providing available to your clients or guests. Assessing the outgoing referrals can also help you show that you are totally and completely about your clients. If you feel that your company cannot fully satisfy a certain client—due to some reason that is not neglect—it shows that you hope for the best and trust of potential customers rather than the money that you could earn from them.

Attracting New Clients

Now, we know it is very important to establish strong relationships with the clients that we start off with, but you can't forget the fact that you are trying to expand your business. Attracting new clients is one of the most important things that you should worry about when it comes to your business and its success.

But what is the best way to get new clients?

Well, when you are struggling to gain new clients, the first thing you should do is assess your social media and networking success. Making sure that people are actually seeing your posts and keeping track of the like and dislikes on those posts is a great way to make sure that the word of your business is actually getting out there. You can check how many people see your post on most admin accounts on most social media. When you see that there is a small number of people seeing your posts, you must find other means to get your information out there.

You can now form groups on the Internet and make sure that the news of these groups gets out. Having groups can allow potential clients to ask others how they feel about the services that you provide. This will help them make the decision of whether or not they want to invest in what you are selling.

Make sure to gather up information and ideas for marketing strategies. Other than what we already have now—inbound marketing—you can decide how you want to get your business out there. This can include asking people to do product reviews, testimonials, and writing blogs. Guest blogging on other people's websites is something else that your copywriters and editors can do. This will help you gain readers on your blog and therefore a better chance to get more customers.

Research is also important. Keeping your research up to date by connecting with other companies, listening to clients, and hiring people to do research and update the business plan yearly, every six months or even quarterly is something that you should think about. Why do all this work, though? You had a business plan; that's good until you meet your goals, right? Wrong! Technology is changing daily, new things are invented, and people find something new to want or need everyday. Keeping your research updated will give you a chance to update your business plan and change it accordingly.

Keeping archives of everything that your business has done in the past and the results from those actions is something else that you should be doing regularly. This could include any business actions like promoting services on Instagram versus Facebook. Keeping records of all of these things can help you maintain a good idea of what works well when attracting new customers and what does not work so well. Along with coming up with new strategies, you can cycle out those old ones, adding a little twist to the idea.

For example, adding promotions like contests for free or discounted services can be done every month or two to attract people and draw attention to your business. You may do this every month or so, but once a year you could do a big giveaway to a random Facebook or Instagram follower. Cycling these two strategies will help you gain more followers, subscribers, and in turn more business for your company or organization.

Get Your Name Out There!

Now you should try to get the company name and service out there! This can be done in many ways. Promoting your business can include some of the many things that we have already talked about and you are familiar with many of them, I'm sure, by now. These things can include copywriting content for a blog, posting advertisements, and promoting events like giveaways and competitions. They are all things that you can do that will surely get your services out there so people can take advantage of them.

You should also make sure that you have a strong brand that you are happy with. Know that making sure that your employees and workers are all aware of the brand and are pleased with it. This may go without saying but depending on the size of your company, it may be difficult to please everyone. There should be a board of officials or partners that can help make decisions. I digress. Your brand should include a logo, tagline, website, and other things like accounts and groups. All of these things help create the image and help you with your need to attract customers and make people aware of what your company is all about.

Going to community gatherings and fairs will also give you the chance to interact with future companies and will allow you to promote your business and inform many people that your business is unknown to them. You could even pass out pamphlets, prizes, and discounts to get people started! This will be sure to help you get some more customers.

Social media offers some of the most powerful tools of this time. Here you can make sure that people of the World's most interactive demographic can hear about your business and spread the news of your promotions. Social media is also great for getting feedback. It provides a great way for people to leave comments and share their opinions. You can also post questions, statements, and, as we've already talked about, promotions and giveaways. On your social media accounts, you can promote your own blogs or other content, this way people can get word of most or all of your content uploads from a bus of their phones!

Creating Effective Communication

When you have a business, there are many different groups that you want to make sure that you keep in good communication with throughout your marketing journey. This includes, most importantly, your workers. Of course, client communication is very important but when it comes to services, you want to be able to make sure that you and your workers have established a good relationship so that they can go to you when they need help with anything they may be struggling with. You do not want to lose customers because your employees do not know what to tell the clients.

That brings us to the clients. When a client has a question, they should get an answer as quickly as possible. Many of us know, as the world is very service oriented, that being left without answers when it comes to a business that we are investing in can be quite annoying and just plain, plump frustrating. So it is important that you make sure that customers can get help, and the customer representatives are kind, patient and informed on what to do and where to go when they are stumped. Keeping an archive of frequent customer questions is also a good idea. When you keep getting the same question over and over again, maybe you should educate your employees on these troubles, get them to explain things a little better, or even put a "Q and A" page on your website. This way if people have questions they can go get answers for themselves.

While you are adding pages to your website, adding a "Contact Us" page is something that you should have on there. This is very important because if people do not know how to contact customer service in times of trouble, they will just leave your services for someone who will help them get answers, Of course, you could imagine that this is very understandable. Not knowing things can be frustrating and frustration is not something that you want when it comes to business transactions. You want everything to go as smooth as possible.

Benefits of Local Inbound Marketing

Even though many of the benefits of inbound marketing that we discussed in the earlier chapter can be carried over to the benefits of local inbound marketing, there are still some advantages you should be aware of that may make you look at local inbound marketing a second time.

First of all, local inbound marketing gives you a chance to connect to the community on a personal level—not just an electronic one.

Going to local fairs, holiday functions, and other events will give you the chance to contribute in ways that not only other businesses will admire, but the people of that general location. This will help build trust, gain respect, and allow your business to be spread by "word of mouth."

Another thing that you could expect is a larger client population. Once you have been in this area for a while and you have familiarized the people and the surrounding area with your services, you may find that people prefer to come to you rather than get that same service online. Even though the Internet is doing wonders for you right now—spreading the word about you services or products—there are some instances where online substitutions for services "simply won't cut it" (meetingking.com). These days the Internet has proven wonderful for overseas video conferences and even doctor's appointments— yes... doctor's appointments. More and more people are transferring to the online world to buy their clothes, makeup, and even groceries along with making their optometrist dentist, and, as stated before, their doctor's appointments.

Despite all of this, there are things that you just cannot do over a video camera. Sometimes, you just have to meet with the service provider in person, and some people still prefer to do that; the older population, for example. Some elderly people struggle with many online services, like banking, so they decide to go to the bank themselves. It all makes sense.

Other than that, face-to-face meetings have many other advantages. This includes a better understanding of the subject that you are talking about. For instance, you may be having a consultation for some sort of service, like a tattoo, piercing, or even a home renovation. In these instances, it is best to have the client meet you in person so that you can discuss plans and they can show you anything that they may feel that may not work for them. You may also find you need to deliver sensitive news; something that must be hard for the client to hear. This kind of information should involve face to face interaction so that you (the service provider) can comfort the client if it is needed. Doing this will help you earn respect and trust from your customers.

Something else that you can expect from meeting with clients in real time is getting people's full attention. When you talk to them online through emails or messages, you don't know if you are getting their full attention. For all you know, on the other end of your online conversation, the person could be dealing with things they may feel are more important. On the flip side, though, if you have that person in the office and you have their full attention, you can make sure that they get all the important information that they need to.

Being able to spread the word about your blogs, websites or past works is another advantage that you can look forward to when practicing local inbound marketing. You have the chance to not only spread your business online but the chance to spread the word about your service by word of mouth of the town's people.

Tips for Local Inbound Marketing

If you are new to inbound marketing, for sure, you could use some tips for local inbound marketing. So here are some of the best things that you could do to be as successful as you dream of becoming while practicing local inbound marketing!

The first thing I want to talk about is something that I cannot stress too much. We've talked about it multiple times throughout the short time that we've spent together; blogging. Maintaining a blog is an important aspect of any type of inbound marketing, not only local inbound marketing. Creating and updating the blog regularly will be the best thing that you can do to attract customers and create awareness.

When you make your website, you could make sure that it is attractive. We've talked about having a clean, smooth website but having a pretty website is just as important as having a properly functioning one. A website that is plain and difficult to navigate is—most of the time—is seen as a waste of time as it causes frustration and is an inconvenience to many customers. So my advice to you is to make your website as appealing and easy to navigate as possible because, I don't know about you, but the cleaner the website, the more pleasant my experience is.

One last tip for your website would be to make your website mobile accessible. Many people have made the move from desktops and laptops to tablets with keyboards. This means that mobile accessible websites are a must have for many people. And it's not only young students who are making these changes. More and more elderly people are learning how to use technology and older adults are indulging in what they never had as children. So making your website mobile accessible will not only attract a young audience but bring you into touch with even the older adult population if you are going for that.

Something that we've already talked about briefly as well is having good researchers. You want to stay on top of things and you want to make sure that your research is up to date and that it is thorough and effective. To do the best research that you can, you should make sure that you, as well as your researchers, are informed on the exact goals that you have for the future and that you know exactly what to do to get there. Research keywords and explore the tips, advice, and even the strategies that other businesses have benefited from to enhance your marketing experience and get leads and customers.

You should also know your audience well. Be aware of what your demographic likes and what they usually like to buy as of right now. This is where your detailed research comes in as well. Make sure that you have a good idea of what your target audience wants. For example, you are not going to target very many young people with denture cleaner, if you know what I mean. Do the research, and learn what your audience wants and what they need. You may find that there are a lot of young people investing in fizzy bath bombs, lip scrubs, and other body cosmetic items right now. On the other hand, you may find that older adults close to retiring are enjoying more outdoor activities like kayaking, fishing, and other outdoor pleasures. Knowing this can help you decide what you want to sell and who you want to advertise to if you have not already done so.

Chapter Three: Content Marketing

So now we know the basics of both inbound and local inbound marketing, but there is another type of marketing that is quite similar if not virtually the same as inbound marketing. This kind of marketing is called content marketing. Content marketing "involves the creation and sharing of online material" with the intent of promoting a product and/or services. So just by looking at the definition, you can see that inbound marketing and content marketing are quite similar.

When people use content marketing, they distribute information and promote their services or products by sharing videos, posting blog or vlogs, and posting e-books and other media via the Internet.

Content Marketing vs. Inbound Marketing

As with inbound marketing, content marketing is fairly new and has become very popular in recent years. But there is a large debate going on about the major differences—if any—between content and inbound marketing. In fact, writtent.com describes this debate "as one of the fiercest marketing debates today". When searching this topic, you'll find many opinionated and biased articles on what people are thinking about these two marketing strategies.

We know that the Internet became most popular in the mid-1990s, and before that, the news was spread by "snail mail"—as many call it—or postage, news, and newspapers. This was the old method or outbound marketing, as we've talked about in previous chapters. Now when the Internet began to spread and was used in many more homes around the world, inbound marketing and content marketing began to take off. This was due to the fact that more and more people were beginning to understand how the Internet works, and employers and business owners would be able to advertise and many of the sites that they knew people used. They "realized that this Internet thing was going to be huge."

So of course, they took advantage of it and began to do their research and essentially learned how to turn marketing around and make it possible for people to earn more respect from companies by letting the people go to the companies for more information. It was sort of like a teasing game. Companies put out just enough information, and people wanted to know more. This became more and more popular as the '90s turned into the 2000s. Eventually, the older outbound strategies were hated and the newer inbound and content strategies were beloved by both business owners and their customers. There was no more badgering or annoying emails, phone calls, texts, or promotions coming through the mail, either. Now people could choose whether or not they wanted to know more.

But what is the real difference between the two strategies? They sound pretty similar and you can tell the story of one strategy while telling the other, but is there really any difference?

Inbound Marketing

We can examine the differences between the two strategies by exploring the two strategies up close. Since we know a lot about inbound marketing already, let's start with that one.

Inbound marketing was defined by HubSpot co-founder Brian Halligan in 2005. He developed the idea and about a year later, it was being written about in articles on HubSpot, giving advertisers and even the greenest of business people the chance to jumpstart their businesses.

It took about a decade to perfect but inbound marketing's just as we've talked about: getting people to come to you. It was never about pushing your content on people, and making them like it or buy; the goal wasn't to bully strangers into becoming buyers. It's always been about attracting strangers and them becoming promoters.

Content Marketing

People believe that content marketing was first used back in 1895 by a Mr. John Deere. You may know this name from a successful modern outdoor equipment company that sells engines, heavy equipment, machinery and the everyday outdoor equipment made or things such as lawn care and maintenance and outdoor camping activities. If you do a Google search on the company you'll see that the founder was a Mr. John Deere.

Back in the day, John Deere would promote deals and small promotions to "provide value to their customers." They would often give out free content or information so that their customers could learn more about their products. For example, they use to give out free advice for farming and using the equipment. Other Companies soon followed suit, giving out free recipe books, comic books, and sponsoring certain shows, movies and books.

Content marketing was all about earning trust and respect without pushing your product on the customers. The goal was to get people to come to you because they wanted to know more.

Brands were also dealing with the fact that people just didn't trust in paid advertising anymore; it was easily seen as biased. If you think about this, it makes sense. If a company is paying someone to say that a product is good... Do I need to say more? They are going to say it's good no matter what. Wouldn't you? If you don't say the product is working, you won't get paid! So the information wasn't real and people found that they were wasting their money. This strategy began to plummet in popularity and no one wanted to invest in anything without a guarantee.

So now people were giving "samples"—in a way—in order for customers to gain their trust and see for themselves if the product is right for them at the moment. This way they do not waste their money.

The Core Differences

So what exactly are the differences between the two marketing strategies? Well, the main difference that we can see is that inbound marketing is almost strictly the use of the Internet. Inbound marketing came into the marketing business way after content marketing did and it was almost solely because people were noticing that they can use the Internet to attract new buyers. However, people have been using content marketing to do that for over a century by the time that inbound marketing became an official thing!

So the biggest difference is that inbound marketing is newer and that it relies on a more modern technology. In other words, inbound marketing is a new and improved content marketing.

Content marketing often focuses on the "creation and distribution of content across multiple channels." This would imply that it is not solely focused on using the Internet to do it—even though it is one of the best ways to get information out there. People use television, magazines, and books to advertise. You often see that at the end of a book there is an excerpt (maybe the first chapter) of the next book there. It gets you excited for the next one and makes you want to buy it a little more, right? You also see that in the pages of a magazine or newspaper, there are coupons or promotions for certain products. This could include a free product if you bring the magazine or enter a certain code on a website.

All of these things combine to reinforce the fact that content marketing is something that you can find in other places—not just the Internet.

Now, we can contrast that with the ever so slightly different inbound marketing. When we talk about inbound marketing, we usually focus on the creating of content on a website to attract buyers, right? That's what we've been discussing since you picked up this book! We already know that inbound marketing is very Internet base—even local inbound marketing. This helps us really pin point the biggest difference between content and inbound marketing.

So at first glance, you would think that the two are the same thing, but now you should be able to see the biggest difference. When you look at the two definitions side by side, the difference may be a little difficult to see; it just takes a little bit of cross examination to see that the two are not the same.

Are there any more differences? The answer is yes!

The next big difference that you should notice is the idea that they work together to do a few different things. While inbound marketing is helping to make your website great to attract action from visitors online, content marketing can help you get those visitors in the first place.

Making your website attractive using web designers, copywriters and editors can help you compel people to actually buy your products or services and drive people to promote your business. But you need to get those people to come in the first place. You can do this by offering free content as a promotion or "first time buy" sort of thing in order to gain the trust and respect of your products. Meanwhile, you can be using the inbound strategy to add pages to the websites where people can apply to promote your product for a price. You pay them to get the name of your services out there—like we've discussed before.

In a nutshell, these two strategies could—and should—be used together in order to optimize your business experience, help your sale skyrocket, and help you make more money.

Benefits of Content Marketing

As we did for inbound and local inbound marketing, let's look at some benefits that we can look forward to experiencing when using the content marketing strategy. There are many of them, so buckle up!

First, you'll find that you will have more content to put on your website. If you have promotions going on and "the first time buy" deals like we stated above, you'll notice that your site will become a little busier. Now, this could be a good thing and it could be a bad thing. It could be a bad thing because you don't want your site to become cluttered and disorganized. However, when you have a good web team and a good designer, you can keep your website spick and span and you will have a lot of content and pages that visitors can explore.

If you have a higher website content, you can also look forward to a higher visibility in search engines. Also when you have free content out there that people are looking for, they will find it a lot easier if the promotions are also advertised on websites from magazines and books. Overall there is just a better chance of someone finding you on the wide, and vast space that is the Internet.

Content marketing also helps build your brand. When you have a better-known brand you're just going to get more business! For example, if you have ads in the back of books, in magazines, and on the Internet, the news of your website gets out. This leads to more Google searches, and more people find your website. Soon enough you're getting lots of people finding out about your products and services and more and more purchases are being made.

The cost is actually going to be a little less. Just like inbound marketing, there is a big dip in costs when it comes to putting your information out there. It doesn't require mass emails, phone calls, texts, and posting (mail). It is often just the idea of making a phone call or email to a magazine company or a book publishing service and their cost of an ad. You could also use the Internet! Remember even though content marketing didn't start off on the Internet, you can use the Internet to do what you need to do. Offering free recipes online or free excerpts from e-books is a great way to gain respect and trust from your clients and get your sales to increase.

You also build a better, closer relationship with your customers. They see that you care for them and their business when they see that you trust them enough to come back and ask questions. For instance, when you have a customer that is uncertain on whether or not they want to buy your product, you can offer them free samples or some sort of free service to help them decide if it is worth their money or not. This will allow the opportunity for direct contact and help build a strong relationship where the client can trust your company.

Content marketing can also help your company generate more leads in general. In fact, it has been proven that content marketing has increased inbound traffic and leads by a whole 54%! That's a big chunk change, is it not? This means that you may also find that using content marketing paired with content rich websites (lots of blogs and videos) can help attract more leads. This is because when people go to your website, they actually have something to look forward to!

You may also find that when you use content marketing, you will be easily established as a good leader of your company. Remember, you are the company; what people think of the business that you are building is what they think of you. For instance, you might be surprised at what people would think of someone who is running a charity. Even though this person may be a scumbag—someone who is only doing what they do to get good publicity—they will most likely be seen as a kind, giving person.

The same goes for someone who runs a bad business. If the business is messy and the workers are grumpy and cranky all the time, people are going to think the same of you! Because content marketing is based on the sampling or "giving some things away for free" aspect, well people are going to see you as a good leader; someone who respects their customers. People will also—most likely—listen to what you want to say. They might see you as a better spokesperson and actually head your words with a little bit of contemplation.

Using this type of marketing may also mean that people come back! When they try out your products and like it they may come back for the second time to buy your products again! This is because they've had the chance to get the product and give it a shot. After trying it—and loving it—they go back and buy the real thing!

Not only can this type of marketing give you a better reputation, but it can also help enhance promotions! People like to share posts, they give each other advice. If your product works, and people begin to love it, they'll post about it! Beauty gurus will talk about it on their Youtube channels and you will gain a social media status that gets you noticed.

How to Create a Content Marketing Strategy

Even though we have a good idea of what the content strategy is, we don't really have a good grasp on how to use it to our advantage. So let's have a look at the steps to creating a content marketing strategy that you can be sure is going to enhance your sales and make sure that your business takes off!

What is your goal?

This should be the first thing that you and your team define before you carry on with anything. Your goal should be something that you find is realistic, something you can see your company accomplishing within the next decade, few years, or even months. People say that long term goals are the best thing to aim for due to the idea that you become more excited or "amped up" about when you get closer. However, small goals are great too, as you can achieve a bigger goal in steps; it helps make one big, daunting goal seem a little less scary.

But what goals should you aim to reach? Well, there are many things that a company can accomplish, depending on the service that they provide. You may decide that you want to donate money to a certain charity or charitable organization by a certain year. For example, you may be selling reusable water bottles. A company that exists today, actually, sells the bottle and gives so much of the proceeds to a family that cannot get access to good drinking water. You may want to save up so much of the money you get each year and donate it in a lump sum, maybe five years from your break even point. There are many things that you can think of when it comes to goals.

A good idea for goals could also include the progression of your company, not so much the charitable donations. You may have the hope to hit your break even point within two years. This could be difficult for a lot of business. For instance, when you open a store, for the first five years, you may be putting a lot more money into the store than you are actually making from it. This is very common and you shouldn't worry if it takes your business to take a while to get going. However, you can make goals and do certain things to help make your business produce more sales a little quicker and "get the ball rolling."

Something else that you may want to do is talk with your team. They may have ideas of what the company should accomplish. It is a good idea to include your team in some goals and make sure that everyone is heard. Of course, as we talked about in the first chapter, as a business grows, it may be difficult to please everyone. But when the company is small, you can make sure that your main team is informed of what the idea is at the end of the day, and make sure that everyone is aware of what the main goal is in the end.

Find Out Your Target Audience

So far, we are seeing a few of the same steps that we heard in the inbound marketing section of this book, so now you can see that there are a lot more similarities than differences between the two marketing strategies.

Finding your target audience, as we know it extremely important and usually isn't that difficult when it comes to selling a product or service. You can develop the product before fitting the demographic to the product or you can determine what kind of people you want to sell to and then come up with a product or service that will help people in that age group, ethnicity, religion, or race.

For instance, you may say to your team "Let's come up with an acne medication that works effectively and can be a quick fix for people!" Once you get in the groove, and you've invented the actual product, it's time to decide on packaging. Well, the packaging is kind of important because you want something that is going to attract the audience that you want to sell your product to... but who do we want to sell to? This is where research comes in. You'll find that "an estimated 80%" of all teenagers and young adults (people from ages 11 to 30) experience acne problems. So you create a colorful, bright packaging that will attract a lot of people, but mostly young adults. I don't know about you, but when I was a teen, I would go for the pretty packaging.

You may go a different route, though; you may have the idea to base the product off the demographic! When you do this, the idea will be to come up with a demographic, for example, elderly people, and come up with a service that they may make use of. So maybe you could have a care facility or a home care business. Your website would be full of profiles that people can examine and look over to determine the best nurse, or professional to take care of themselves or their loved ones.

Coming up with the key demographic should not be a big problem if you pay attention to what is trending on the Internet, or what is really advertised on television or in books and magazines.

Run an Audit

Yes; run an audit! Why not?

"What's an audit?" Well, an audit is when someone carries out a full "official inspection" of an organization to see how it works. However, we want to think about an audit a little differently. We want to run a "content audit", meaning we want to look at other people's blogs and posts, and see if it is similar to what we want to post. For example, you may see that many of the cute, colorful websites with blogs that have lots of pictures are getting a lot of views and reads. Knowing this, adding lots of colors, animations, "gifs" and pictures to your blogs will help spice up the website and attract more people.

However, you do not—I repeat—do not want to copy these sites and blogs. This is plagiarism and it is illegal. You can lose your business and be given a hefty fine for doing it. So what you want to do is use the ideas that they have come up with—like the layout of their blog—and create your own little twist to it. This will help make your website unique but, at the same time, what everyone likes.

When you fit in too much, though, you may disappear amongst all of the nonsense that you can find on the Internet. Make sure that you use a unique name, website, or idea of your own that makes you stand out from the crowd.

Manage Your Content

Make sure that you have a system in place so that you can manage your content easily. This will allow you to have a good hold on when you uploaded last when you should upload again, and whether or not people are enjoying what you're uploading.

You should have people for this, as well. Even though you have copywriters and editors and you have people to look after your website and its functionality, but do you have people to look after your content and keep you updated on how many likes, dislikes, and shares that your blogs or videos get? You should! This could even be your job! You'll want to keep an eye and take a note of what people like the most. This way you will know what to post more of and what to not post anymore.

Something else that you can keep track of is the content that brings people in. You need to know not only what keeps people around. You want to attract new people and keep the older subscribers and clients. So it is very important to make sure that you know what is pulling people in, what is keeping them, and what is driving people away from your website.

Chapter Four: What Kind of Content is there to Publish?

Since you started this book, you've read about how important content is to your website when it comes to inbound marketing, but *what is there to publish*?

Forms of Content

Blogs

Blogs are becoming more and more popular. They are seen as opportunities for readers to learn more about certain subjects and a way for writers to improve their writing, thinking and broaden their knowledge of how the social world works.

There are many benefits to blogging, other than the above mentioned and the obvious attraction of people to your website. This includes getting money on just the blog alone! Depending on how many people see your blog and what people think of it, you can make somewhere between pennies a year and thousands of dollars a year. This is a great option for companies who are just getting started, as they can gain ad revenue and make money almost right away; even if no one is buying their product.

Of course, a blog is a good way to present a call to action and to promote. When you blog you can even blog about your product and its benefits. Blogging is also free. There are tons of websites that you can use—if not your own—to post your blogs. Even Google has a blogging site, where people can post whatever they like, design their own blogging page and help people get on their feet with their blog.

Webinars

Once your company has money and can support web interaction, it may be a good idea to give webinars a shot. So you know what a seminar is, I assume. If not it is basically a meeting between organizations to discuss a certain subject. Seminars are often open to the public, but many people only go if they are interested in the subject or if they are part of the organization.

You may have attended seminars in college or university with you class mates as a part of a course that you did, or you may have heard of seminars that were being offered in a field that interested you and your co-workers or peers.

A webinar is simply a seminar that is conducted over the Internet.

Just like blogging, there are free services that you can use in order to get your webinar up on the Internet. Most times, webinars are live but are also recorded for others to watch them later. In fact, Google does have service called Google+ Hangouts where you can create and host a webinar from your office—if you wanted to.

Webinars are best for people who feel that they are very good at public speaking and think that they can win over customers by providing information in such a way that people want to know more. The idea is always the same, though; get people to come to you!

Using your website, you can inform your visitors of your webinar's time and website, any passwords or codes they may need to enter, and what the webinar will be about. Once you have everything set up, you can easily stand infant of the camera and talk away. There are often live chats so that people can ask questions as you go, so communication is not lost and everyone still has a chance to get their voices heard.

Surveys

Surveys are also a great way to get people to understand or even just hear about your product. Conducting free optional surveys is one of the best ways to hear what they people are saying about your business and help you pick out the things that need to be improved, added, or taken away.

From surveys, you can gather the information and data that they've collected and find a way to analyze it so that you can find everything that you need. Some business conduct surveys every few years, while other companies ask every customer they have to fill out a survey.

A good example of this is the banking company The Bank of Nova Scotia. When you go to one of their officers and ask for financing help, you give them an email address. Later that day, you may get an email asking you to fill out a five to ten question survey to see how their workers did. The company does this so that they can get a handle on which workers are doing the best, which ones need help, or just how their company is working in general.

Memes

For those of us in the older generation, you may not have heard of the Internet phenomenon "memes." Memes are described as funny, cringe-worthy, or silly animated and captioned pictures that make fun of some sort of trend, population, celebrity and more.

Because they are sometimes rude and may even "poke fun" at certain groups or individuals, it is very easy to offend someone when it comes to these silly pictures. So you are cautioned to be very careful and make sure that you are going very easy on the jokes when it comes to something that may offend someone.

User Generated Content

User generated content is a great way to get people involved in your cause. User generated content marketing is actually a very successful marketing strategy and is used by companies such as Starbucks, Belkin, and Target.

User generated content is the stuff that is created on your website made by people who actually are not getting paid. Think of it as a donation. Sometimes consumers of your product can actually generate this content by writing blogs on your website about your service and more. User generated content can include blogs, vlogs, e-books, videos, pictures, and anything else under the sun that you can turn into something that people can enjoy.

A lot of companies do this, as it makes them look good, bringing their customers in on the secrets, allowing them to post about their products for free and not having to worry about copyrights or any bad impact it may have on their finances curata.com says that user content is so effective because it opens the gates to trust and allows customers to value the service and business owners to respect their customers.

Another thing to think about is the fact that people just like to hear from "people like them." In fact, 70% of people would rather see testimonials from "real" people instead of from paid contributors or celebrities. This is because there is less of a chance of biased information.

So when you think about it, user generated content may be a better source of content than you think.

Pictures

It may sound a little childish or juvenile, but people just simply like to see pictures when they read. In fact, 92% of college students like to see pictures in their textbooks.

"A picture says a thousand words" has been a heavily used quote for many years, and it has always bee true. When people read about products, recipes, or even history, they like to see pictures of the actual item or event. This is very common. If you think about it, when you shop online you are not going to buy something if you don't know what it looks like; even when people buy books there is a picture of the cover. Aren't we not suppose to "judge a book by its cover"?

There are many other examples of this, if that one is too weak, as it may be a bit of a stretch. When people have a recipe book or blog, they want to see pictures of the actual dish once it is finished. This is because if it doesn't look any good, people do not want to make it! It's simple fact!

Pictures are just important for a lot of people; myself included.

Tips for Online Content Publishing

Making sure that the content that you post is going to actually attract people is very important, as it would be the whole purpose of you publishing the content. So what you want to do is educate yourself on what you can do to make sure that your content is public-ready. Here are some tips to help you do that!

First off, you want to make sure that your content is actually correct. Publishing false content can get you in trouble and cause you to lose the business and respect that you are working so hard to get. So to help build—and keep—your reputation, please make sure that your content is true, as far as your knowledge can take you, anyway.

Secondly, make sure you have a copyright statement that protects you and your writers. Just in case something is wrong, you will not be able to be used if your copyright warning is true and detailed; you can never be too detailed. The copyright statement will help you and your workers be completely protected just in case someone follows your advice and becomes sick or injured. For example, if you are writing about exercise and dieting. If someone hurts themselves following your advice or if someone gets sick following your diet, your copyright notice can protect you.

The copyright notice also interferes with anyone that may try to steal your work. When you've worked hard on something, you obviously wouldn't want someone to just copy and paste it on their site, would you? I think not!

When you have the copyright notice, you can actually sue someone for plagiarizing your work. This can help you save money and stop people from wrongfully making the money that you should get credit for.

Now onto the actual content tips.

Posting unique content can help you stand out from the crowds. If you have something in your blogs or videos that no one else does, you are going to seem different and cool amongst all the other people who are creating content right next door.

You may want to be detailed, as well. A lot of people hate doing research. If they are trying to find something out about a certain subject or field, they like to look at the smallest amount of pages and websites as possible. It can become tiring to sit in front of the computer for hours trying to find all the information that you possibly can on a certain subject.

So you, as the writer, or your copywriters, may want to provide as much information as possible in order to please all those people who come across your website. When you have a well-informed audience, they may come back later to find something else that they cannot find elsewhere.

Having a grammatically correct article is something else that you will see is very important. People want to understand what is being said and they do not want to have to focus on it too much to try and figure out what you're trying to say.

Even having some sort of grammar and spell check on your computer when you are writing may be a good idea. The one that many writers use nowadays is Grammarly. Grammarly does not only check for spelling errors, but for structural and grammatical errors that you may have made throughout your article. Of course, it is hard to forget that you are just human and you make mistakes; you are not a computer. Sometimes small errors will get past you, but it's not that big of a deal, as long as your article is understandable.

Having tone and a certain style is also important. When you have a tone of voice in your writing it helps people understand you better, and see where you are coming from. Sometimes it is so easy to tell which emotion an author is feeling when they are right. You could sense a happy or content tone, or you can feel anger or annoyance in some of their works without the author even mentioning how they are feeling.

So you should keep this in mind when you are writing your own content, as you do not want people getting the wrong idea when they are reading your content; it's very important!

If you develop your own writing style, you should also make sure that you keep it consistent throughout your articles. It's not so bad if you change it from one article to the next, but you want to make sure that you use on writing style at the beginning of a blog and then a different writing style near the middle and end. This can confuse the reader and disrupts the flow and discipline of the paper or article.

If you are interested, you may want to begin on a free website first. This will give you the chance to make some money and still get some recognition from the online community. When you finally have enough money to make your own website and hire people to help you out with things, then you can let everyone know that you are making the move to your own website. Talk about all the features you may have and may even self-promote a little bit. This will attract people and help you keep the customers you have while gaining a few new ones!

You also want to make sure that you have a comments section for your content. This is very important because you want to have lots of conversation and flow to your website. When people have an issue, they can simply comment it on the forum so that you can see it right there. This saves you the trouble of searching through hundreds of emails to find one question. If someone comments a question or concern, there is also the advantage that people that have the same issue will be able to see your reply! Now you don't have to answer the same question over and over again!

Don't forget the search engines! Make sure that you have key words in your titles that have a lot to do with the article and that are being searched regularly. Usually, it is a good idea to put at least one of the "five w's": who, what, when, why and how. This is usually the started word of many of the searches in google today.

Partner with magazines and other websites. They can spread the news and advertise your blogs and other content in an attempt to get people to come to your website more often. Having your article published in the newspaper or a magazine can help you tons when it comes to getting your work out there. Of course, this will also help you get more traffic and visitors to your website.

Having multiple websites or having your work featured on multiple websites may also be a good idea. Early in this chapter, we also talk about starting off on free websites, what makes you think that you can't stay on the free one, and have your own paid website? Even though it may be a few hours of extra work if you can do it, why not? It is only going to get more awareness of your services or products and allow for a better opportunity for more people to see your blog.

Making your content available to everyone; including mobile users is something that is super important for many businesses. People get so frustrated—including myself—when their favorite website is difficult to navigate on a cell phone or tablet. The fix for that is to have a mobile version of your website so that people can easily access it on their phones, on the go. This will increase your views and then in turn increase the awareness of sales, and finally, boost sales!

Have checklists, as well. Make sure that you've said all that needs to be said and that you haven't missed anything. It is very important, as I stressed earlier, to have all the information you possibly can in your works, as people like to have everything right infant of them. Having a checklist will allow you say everything you've meant to and to not forget things. If need be there are reminder apps that you can get to help you check everything off the list as you go. This can be helpful when it comes to videos, blogs, articles, e-books, webinars, and even when you are conducting surveys—you don't need to be forgetting important questions.

Youtube is a very popular platform, getting over one billion active users and visitors each month. People come and go as they people, and people have found so much success in their careers from Youtube. Youtube, if you do not know, if a place where you can watch videos, comment on those videos, interact with other viewers and artists, as well as post your own videos; their slogan being "Broadcast yourself."

People are beginning to rather watching over reading due to many reasons, like just not wanting to take the time and read and liking the stronger feeling of human interaction. Your article can have as much voice as possible but it is never going to have the same amount of voice a real person can have.

Sometimes people are just better at listening than reading. Actually, most people read something and only remember 20% of it. Let's contrast that with the extra 10% that people remember when they watch and listen to something. It is just something about the brains of human being that makes them remember more when they watch and listen. This is why, in schools, they are bringing in more videos, movies, and shows that tie into the lesson instead of sticking kids' heads in books all day long.

Along with this, when you are read, a lot of what you read you may not understand. A lot of people—myself included—just read past what the words are saying on the page, space out for a second, and lose half of what they just read.

They have to read that section again. When this happens to people, they often just put down the book and stop reading.

So there are just a few reasons why you should have videos on Youtube and your website that can go along with your blogs. It may be some extra work, but it will definitely be worth it.

Chapter Five: Business to Business (B2B) Inbound Marketing

Since we've started talking about inbound marketing, we have been discussing the idea of starting a business and what you can do to boost your sales and grow your business larger. However, our conversation should not be directed solely towards small businesses.

Have you ever wondered how much money a large corporation would have to have in their possession in order to provide computers to hundreds of employees? Well, they do not do it on their own. When business and large companies supply their workers with—sometimes the most expensive—laptops and desktops, they do not simply "save" their money until they have enough to buy 300 iMac computers. You'd think that they just buy the computers and allow their workers to use them as a courtesy.

Fortunately, it does not work like that at all! Most—if not all—times, business leaders reach out to companies that sell what they need. In return for advertising their logo, the company will allow the other business to get a large discount—or in some cases free—equipment or supplies to help run their business more smoothly. This is called business to business or B2B marketing.

Now, B2B marketing does not have to involve large, expensive items all the time. This may include printers, pens, notepads, pencils, or other office supplies as well as sports equipment or clothing. The smallest of businesses can invest in products from a large corporation or vice versa; it really, truly depends on the company and its willingness to spend or its availability.

So you can see that this method of marketing is quite different from what we've been talking about for the past little while. B2B is not based on the advertising and promoting of a product or service; it is about putting your business into the industry and allowing the company investing in you to do all the promoting for you.

It may seem that a lot of companies, such as Apple Macintosh, could lose quite a bit of money when giving other companies large discounts or free products—especially when they produce such quality, expensive materials. However, when people see that even the most elite of corporations are using certain products, they figure that it is worth investing in.

Keeping up with the explanation of Apple Macintosh, people put their children in what they feel is the best school for their child's need; it's important to them. So when they walk into the school and see that this private school is using Apple Mac computers—laptops and desktops—they feel that the brand is trustworthy.

This may be a little harder to picture because the brand is so well appreciated and respected anyway, but if we look at other brand names; ones that are not as popular at home, but are in the office. Office Depot. This office supply company is used by many different offices across the United States and Canada—and elsewhere in the world. People choose to use these products in their offices because it produces quality products.

When people go to some sort of meeting or consultation in an office building, they see that these respected companies are only using things from the Office Depot. "Why don't I buy some of those things for my kids for school?" or "I could pick up some of these folders of my home office." People start to talk then, and by word of mouth, people are spreading the news about the office depot and their products. Next thing you know the company is bringing in big bucks when back to school comes along, and then all year 'round when people are steadily buying a few things here and there to update their home office supplies.

How to Use Social Media to Promote you B2B

It is said by a few marketing bloggers that B2B is usually boring and people involved in the "stink at social media" (blog.kissmetrics.com). So with this in mind, let's see if you can change the thinking of these bloggers and experts and show that your business can make B2B a little more interesting!

So first off, you want to work on not making your B2B boring. You can start with having an uplifting attitude and try to act as "non-boring" as possible. I know that it sounds silly, but people who know that people think their business is boring, tend to act like it subconsciously. So, the first thing you'll want to do is get that mind set out of your head. This way, you can become less boring in a sense of personality.

Something else you should talk about is the more interesting aspects of some of you more "boring" products. Sometimes when you have a service or product that is viewed publicly as boring, you could explain the more interesting aspect of the product. This will help open the eyes of many people and allow them to get a better idea. Maybe by doing this, you can find a connecting subject that people have a better interest in. A blog on kissmetrics.com sums this scenario up perfectly with a great example.

> "A vivarium misting system help reptiles to survive in an environment that is different from their native environment. It's going to help pythons thrive in a research environment so scientists can understand them. Do you see the unbarring angle emerging?
>
> "There may not be a lot of people interested in vivarium misting systems, but there are a lot of people interested in pythons or rainforest preservation..."

There are no better words to put this into, as the writer says it all, explaining perfectly what I have described in the past few chapters. You need to go about marketing a certain way, which sometimes means thinking outside of the box. It may also mean that you are going to encourage a broader, more diverse audience. Continuing on with the last example, you may find wildlife activists, reptile lovers, animal lovers in general, and environmentalists hidden and poked everywhere within you demographic, when originally, you may have just aimed for animal lovers in the first place.

Once you find an angle that is not boring, you can give your company quite the boost in sales and publicity.

Getting someone to advertise—from the company that you are engaging the B2B with—is another good idea. Having them publicly speak about your product is something that you should ask them to seriously consider. Sponsoring their events, conferences, and more can help you get your name out there, and reach further corners of the marketing world. You may add even more people to the mix in your demographic.

When you find this person, you should make sure that he or she is really good at what they go. As we said, B2Bs try hard, but often do not succeed when it comes to a lot of social media. Not all companies are made by young people, as it takes a long time for a business to get to the point of B2B-ing. Often times, you are seeing an older man—in his 50s or 60s—trying to understand what Twitter is and how he can use it to "hype" up his business's reputation.

Well, maybe you should get a social media expert instead!

It is important that, when it comes to your business, you have the right person, or people, working for you, as sometimes this business could be a little difficult for you and your business. Remember that when you pay for someone to do a job you want to find someone who is worth paying for.

Usually, B2Bs will try to find someone who already has a successful advance in the social media network. This could mean have a high number of followers on Twitter or Instagram or just someone who has a highly respected blog or Youtube channel. The possibilities are almost endless, as there are many people who are simply famous because they're famous—it's almost ridiculous. A lot of famous people are very successful on the social media platforms as well and many of the celebrities that young people look up to today have multiple accounts on multiple different social websites.

Finding someone that is will to share their time and experience with you to enhance your marketing reputation and your business's success is what you're looking for.

And of course, we should through some content in there. Since this is inbound marketing B2B, you should give posting content a shot. You know all the information that you need to on content already; just pick what you think would be the best and easiest for your workers and get to it!

The B2B Funnel

As we've learned in previous chapters, many marketing strategies have some sort of step system for beginners to follow and masters to alter. B2B is no different. As usual, though it has its own little cook name just like marketing has "the fours pillars". Well, B2Bs follow the B2B (inbound) marketing funnel. This "funnel" can be altered to fit into many different kinds of marketing, but since this selection is solely based on inbound marketing and those that are closely related to it, we'll stick with the inbound marketing version.

The B2B funnel is divided into four main steps: attract, convert, close, and delight; in that order. Let's talk about each step in detail.

Your main goal—aside from keeping customers—would be to attract new ones. So this is where the adding of content and promoters come in. If you have any means of advertising now is the time to do it, because you're ready to go and you need customers, right? You can host live streams, shows, commercials, and more to generate a main call-to-action that customers look for; for motivation.

Now, the people that visit your website and hear your call-to-action, you want to make those people—visitors—into customers. With the use of leading pages with enticing, motivating, and reasonable calls-to-action that get the visitor interested. This is the converting step. Does this kind of sound familiar? All of these marketing strategies are very closely related to the original inbound marketing that we started talking about at the beginning of this selection.

For the sake of time and as I try not to be too repetitive, I'll let you fill in the blanks for the Close and Delight stages as they are quite self-explanatory.

So what is this B2B funnel, and how does it work, exactly?

Well, I guess we'll start with what it is used for. The marketing funnel is used to help marketer, usually beginners, to understand and plan their marketing process. The funnel can help provide marketers with guidance at the beginning, middle or end of their marketing journey, each stage providing some sort of advice that people can follow.

Now when we talk about the funnel, think of it a cone shape, wide on the top and narrow at the bottom. Most of the top, a little of 60% of the funnel is dedicated to marketing. This would include the first two stages, while the other two stages—close and delight—are near the bottom of the funnel, symbolizing the closing of a sale and the satisfaction of the customer. They make up the last 30% or so.

You can think of the funnel as an input and output system, you put in your marketing strategies (the ones we've been talking about), causing lead generation. Then, the next stage your strategy would be to convert visitors into customers. Here, your company's inputs are going to be content and entertainment. This will help attract customers and allow people to decide if they want to invest in any of your services or products. Now finally, the close and delight stages. Here your inputs would be "trails and demonstrations" and then out pops the money that you have worked so hard for. Not only will money be a benefit, but you will also see that you have just made a trusting customer that can refer your business to other people.

Another thing that you want to keep in mind—something good, of course—it the fact that the marketing funnel is a cycle. People come back, or new people come in and the cycle starts all over again! Are you starting to see how it works?

You may also see a large connection to the other types of marketing and the use of the funnel with B2B marketing. Even though there are many different kinds of marketing, they are all somehow connected, especially in their goals and initiatives.

Tips and Tricks for B2B Inbound Marketing

When you are putting your faith in something, especially something this important, you should at least be prepared for any failures and such. However, I've compiled a list of tips and tricks that will allow you to avoid failure and help you get the hang of inbound B2B marketing before you even begin the journey!

So the first tip that I have for you is to write a lot of in-depth content! "It's no secret: Google loves in-depth articles" (entrepreneur.com). It could not have been said any better and it cannot be any more clear or right. People just absolutely love to learn a lot about something that they are searching up. I, myself, love to indulge in a long article about something I am interested. This goes for much of the google search community. People always love to know more.

Creating longer, more detailed content will help you gain visitors and eventual customers due to the idea that people just like to be informed on all sides of the story, all angles of the subject, and all theories on the idea.

Recycle content! If you find that you are running out of things to write about and you do not know what to do, you should post tomorrow afternoon or tonight, why don't you try updating an old article. Updating it could mean giving it a few moderations or it could mean rewriting it. Of course, you want to add something to it and change is some way or another instead of just reposting and edit of what you posted 6 months ago.

Something to remember when reposting old content; make sure that you do not do this

Often. It is just a quick fix and is something you want to do only on those occasions where you cannot figure out what to do on a short deadline.

Do not try to start new trends. Instead of trying to be "cool" and find something new to try to get people to do, why don't you just add to what people are already doing? When you think about it, setting trends and trying to get people interested in certain things could be quite difficult and is, in fact, a very unreliable way of doing things. Instead of trying to do something that you might—or almost definitely will—fail at, why don't you just try to go with the flow and figure out a way to "fit in" with the crowd.

This is a little tricky, though, because you want to be different from everyone else... you want to be unique. But how can you do that and stay the same as everyone? Well, the trick would be to create something that is different but helps with something that a lot of people have trouble with in their everyday lives.

For example, I noticed a pack of hair pins that were "no teeth needed". For this of you who do not know, a certain type of hair pin, bobby pins, are very popular all over the world and has been used for centuries to pin hair in certain places. If you've used one of these pins before, you may remember using your teeth to pull apart the two prongs of the clip so that you can slide it through your hair. Well, I saw a pack of Bobby Pins that had a little device attached to the packaging that allowed you to slide the two prongs of the pin apart without using your teeth.

This manufacturer took something very popular and put a little something different on the packaging to make it unique. Speaking from a consumer standpoint, it really caught my eye, and I did, in fact, buy the pins.

You could also update your content every six months to a year to show people that you are updating your research and learning more as your business grows. This also shows that you still care about your customers and viewers. Giving out false information is not what you want to do, as it could drive customers away if they find out—when they find out. So the best thing for you to do it to make sure that you do not have wrong information in the first place, but to update your content every six months from the publish date in order to make sure that your data is trustworthy.

Make sure that your loading times and page speed are at a good pace. You do not want people to leave your website simply because it is slow. So not only should a website be laid out right and pretty, but it should also be fast and smooth so the people can navigate it quickly and efficiently

Chapter Six: What You Need to Know Before You Go

Well, our time is almost up, but there are a few things that you should know about marketing—if it's your first time—before you go about your day. The marketing world can be a cutthroat place, and when it comes to working with big corporations, putting your name out there and giving out information, there are a few things that you should be aware of before you put yourself out there for the Internet and the whole world to see.

Warnings and Advice

First, we'll talk about the things that you should know and things that you should make sure you have—in terms of skills—before you start working in the industry.

You should know that you need to act as a bridge builder. When you become a marketer, you should be aware of the compromises and negotiations that you will have to make with many different people. Not only will customers want to negotiate, but other businesses, workers, and even people in your inner circle are going to have something that they want to change when it comes to your business. So instead of screaming and yelling at people to go about their merry way, you should learn how to make deals, which deals are the most beneficial to you, and how to make and close them properly.

Learning how to negotiate effectively is something else that you should read up on. Trying to argue with much larger, more successful companies is something that you are going to have to face and it's not always easy. There are things that you need to know; things that you can find easily on the Internet.

If you are arguing about budget or prices, always start higher than your goal. If your company says "Let's go for $100 000", tell the other party that you want $200 000 and work your way down. The reason why you want to do this is that you will get what you want while making the arguing party that you are getting less than what you aimed for. This is one of the basic ideas of negotiation.

Something else that you can keep in mind when negotiating is that you should be the on to actually start the argument. Doing this will help you get a little ahead in negotiating and allow you to have the advantage. You can catch a lot of people off guard when you make the first move because of the simple fact that everyone thinks that you won't want to make the first move; especially when you are a small company.

When you go into the marketing business, sometimes you have to be selfish. Thinking of only you and your company is something that is very important. You kind of have to act like a lawyer. You have to turn off your emotions sometimes. This is what makes marketing so difficult for some people. Having a conscience may make the business a little difficult. Marketers sometimes have to push back their connections to the people that they are beating and just lift their head high and rip off the Band-Aid.

This will also help you with another very important aspect of marketing; power. You need to be seen as powerful and strong. Walking away from a fight because you're afraid to hurt someone's feelings may be what will break your business down into a million pieces. You have to understand that power is imperative in marketing and without it, you may not survive. If you survive and your business prevails, you will be pushed around like a ball in the grass.

Showing that you are passionate about what you do will also help you seem more powerful. When you would do anything for your business, people will do anything they can to get out of your way before they are steamrolled down and flattened to the ground. Nobody wants to get in the way of a powerful, passionate business owner.

There are many things that you can do to help reinforce the fact that you are a powerful, strong leader, including using eye contact as a way to control people. Telling someone to shut up is most effective with a glare. Other ways of becoming more powerful in the eyes of everyone else is to make them feel big or good about themselves. This can help you gain respect as well as power. People will see you as the boss who is nice to everyone.

You also have to be a bold person when it comes to the marketing industry. When people start to back you into a corner you have to be able to get up, make a move and make them crawl into the other corner. You have to have the guts and the nerves to make big steps and to almost invade someone's personal space or break their limits.

A lot of people say that you should intentionally break to rules. This may show that you are powerful, relentless and that you don't care about the rules and that you will do what it takes to keep your business afloat. Of course, I advise that you have a limit and that no actual laws are broken; you do not need to be getting in trouble.

Using more than one kind of marketing is something else that you should open your eyes to. There are many different kinds of marketing, different strategies, that you can give a shot. You may find that inbound and content marketing work together—as many have in the past—or you may find that you like to collaborate with other business, investing in B2B marketing. There are many things that you can do to make sure that your business is promoted just by exploring and finding out the right marketing for you and your company.

Make sure that you have an original idea. It may seem really simple, but it is overlooked by a lot of businesses. It is so important that you stand out in the crowd and that your business differs from others. When you have an original product and you know that it is different, you know that more and more people are going to like the idea of it. Nowadays, people really like different; people strive to be different. No one wants to blend in and just be "normal". People are starting to discover that "normal" isn't a word that can be used to describe people because no one is normal.

It may seem a little odd to put this after I say get ready to fail, but be ready for success. Even though the business is tough, it has happened where people just got lucky and passed every problem that they encountered without any issue. Luck is a bad word to use, though. Successful corporations like Facebook or Apple were not built just out of luck. They didn't just get lucky. There were millions of man hours put into those business and so much money. That is what you need to do. Don't sit around and wait for success to just come to you; it won't happen. You have to work hard to get to where you want to be.

Last of all you need to be committed. Starting a business is not easy and it takes a lot of time, effort, and money. So you need to be ready to invest your time and capital into this idea. If not, then it's just not worth it. Not being committed means that you're going to lose money when you quite—and trust me, without commitment, you will quit—so you might as well not start if you are unsure that you can actually go through with this.

This business is a bloody battlefield, and you have to be ready.

Things You Need to Do

Just as there are warnings that you need to heed before you go into the marketing industry, there are also things that you need to do; there are things that you have to prepare and get it set in place.

First of all, you should be aware of the other businesses in your vicinity that are similar to yours. If you have a small business and the location that you've decided for you headquarters is surrounded by large corporations that will cut your business in half and service it to their customers, then you should rethink your location.

You should be aware of what is selling really well, also. If there are a lot of hair products selling currently, but you can see that in the next few years people are going to be wanting something else, do not go straight for what is selling right now. By the time you get on your feet and actually start making money, the trend may have passed and people might have found something new. That would be mean the re-planning and re-thinking of most of your business. So skip that whole ordeal and go straight for the future.

You should also make sure that you have built a business plan that has been perfected over and over again. This will ensure that you will have a solid plan that has no holes, no issues and you will not have to second guess yourself anymore.

Speaking of second guessing yourself, it may be a good idea to do that before you start as well. If you've made a certain decision, it might actually be a good idea to think about whether or not it is a good one. The same goes for when you change your mind about something. Your teachers in school might have said to never change your answer after you've circled that letter, but now we're about to completely change your whole thinking about that.

In business, second guessing yourself is seen as a precautionary. You should think about it first before you change your idea because of the simple fact or what could have been. If you had a good idea, it looked good and then you had a different one, you might change it and then all of a sudden, the business next store is rolling in the business and cash while you picked the wrong marketing strategy or the wrong product to sell.

This industry means big sacrifices and a high chance of losing, so you have to be as prepared as you possibly can to accept any losses or failures that may come your way.

You should start your research right away. This will help you discover your exact goals and what you should decide to sell. Researching things that are trending right now, what people think will be trending in the future, and others along those lines can definitely help you in the long run and save you time and money.

Earlier, we talked about having a checklist when you are putting your content together to make sure that you won't miss or forget anything. Well, you should also have a "before you start" checklist. This will ensure that you have all of your things in order before you really commit to launching your startup.

Talk to someone who you think can help. If that means that you have an uncle or aunt in business that you think can help, go for it! If it means that you just want to talk to a friend and ask them to help you weigh the pros and cons, well do that, too. You need to make sure that you have talked to someone about your ideas to make sure that they seem realistic. Having an outside opinion may also be a good opportunity for reassurance and some guidance when it comes to your business. You may have also just gained someone to talk to when you are unsure about something.

You should also get a lawyer. This may be an expense, but be prepared for something to go wrong. Having a lawyer is a must haves, even for small businesses. If something goes wrong and someone steals your content or you steal theirs, you going to want a lawyer to help you understand what exactly is going on and how to fix it.

Finances

Now, your finances are very important. When you are about to invest a lot of money into something so big and important, you should make sure that you have a lot of money to back you up in case something happens. This means that you should have a good amount of money in a savings account when you start marketing; just in case.

The main thing that you need to do, is separate your personal and business finances. Unless you've raised money for your business, you should not have to dip into any personal bank accounts for your business. This helps protect you, your family, and your business. The best thing that you could ever do is to have separate bank accounts—separate banks, even—for your business and home finances.

You're going to want to start by realizing that if you are using personal bank accounts and funds to deal with the business' finances, you could be held personally liable for the bills, debts, and problems if something ever goes wrong. It is called piercing the corporate veil and you should avoid doing it so that you will not be bothered at home by what going on with the business—relatively.

If you want to avoid piercing the corporate veil, you should start by, as said before, making sure that your accounts are separated and that all your bank statements and records are kept away from your home records.

You can keep your home and work finances separate by opening yourself a business checking or savings account and getting a business credit card. All cards that exist for the business should stay locked up on the actual property with any one or valuables that they business may have.

Conclusion

At its core, marketing is defined as "the study and management of exchange relationships". Even though this is true and marketing is all about creating relationships and exchanging product or service for money, we know now that it is much more than that. Marketing should really be defined as a complicated mess—unless you follow all of the tips and instructions that you found here in this book.

With the help of the Internet, some research and the information that we have been exploring for the past few chapters, you can get your startup to the point where you want it, make money, and not get a headache while doing it.

The key is to be aware of what you need and talk to people. When you talk to people about what you need, maybe you can get some help, and you can never get enough of that.

You'll learn how to master inbound marketing! If won't be long before you are a regular expert when it comes to knowing what down to it and soon enough, you will be helping people with their startup companies. You'll be the one telling people that content is so important and you will have to aid them in understanding exactly how to get the content out there and what to write or share.

Being a social media expert is now the task. Once you get a checklist done up of everything that you need, you can work on communicating and interacting with people, as this will be very important!

Finally, you'll need to be open minded, as marketing is unpredictable and even when you think you know everything, something might come up and smack you in the face before you even realize that it was possible.

Predictability isn't a word when it comes to this business. Good luck.

And finally, if you liked the book, I would like to ask you to do me a favor and leave a review for the book on Amazon. Just go to your account on Amazon to leave a review.

Thank you and good luck!

Resources

https://www.slideshare.net/hungnmhq/32-enviable-inbound-marketing-examples-by-hubspot

http://leadg2.thecenterforsalesstrategy.com/what-is-inbound-marketing

http://www.investopedia.com/terms/s/sales-lead.asp

https://www.usingenglish.com/forum/threads/34042-Who-is-potential-customer

http://www.northstarmarketing.com/marketing-strategist-position-description/

https://blog.hubspot.com/blog/tabid/6307/bid/31271/how-inbound-marketing-works-from-start-to-finish-infographic.aspx

https://www.searchenginejournal.com/unconventional-guide-content-writing-vs-copywriting/114408/

https://hiring.monster.com/hr/hr-best-practices/recruiting-hiring-advice/job-descriptions/web-developer-job-description-sample.aspx

https://hiring.monster.com/hr/hr-best-practices/recruiting-hiring-advice/job-descriptions/marketing-coordinator-job-description-sample.aspx

https://quarizmi.com/blog/is-paid-search-inbound-or-outbound-marketing/

http://www.history.com/topics/inventions/invention-of-the-Internet

http://www.thedailymind.com/stress/blogging-can-help-reduce-stress-improve-wellbeing/

http://www.business2community.com/inbound-marketing/5-key-benefits-inbound-marketing-01241334#fGs3oKQlFDVTOMXV.97

http://www.digitaldistillers.com/blog/5-benefits-of-inbound-marketing-for-your-business

http://meetingking.com/face-to-face-meetings-vs-virtual-meetings/

https://lojomarketing.com/what-is-local-inbound-marketing/

https://www.psm-marketing.com/resources/the-four-pillars-of-marketing/

https://www.forbes.com/sites/jaysondemers/2016/06/02/do-these-5-things-to-master-inbound-marketing/#4f9821605de3

https://www.searchenginepeople.com/blog/5-quick-tips-for-local-inbound-marketing.html

http://fuseboxcreative.ca/beginner-tips-for-local-inbound-marketing-in-moncton/

https://www.hubspot.com/inbound-marketing

http://fuseboxcreative.ca/beginner-tips-for-local-inbound-marketing-in-moncton/

https://www.inc.com/jayson-demers/the-top-10-benefits-of-content-marketing.html

http://www.business2community.com/infographics/8-hard-ignore-content-marketing-benefits-infographic-01038290#eoJGfRtosEJWoZUb.97

http://www.wordstream.com/blog/ws/2017/04/25/benefits-of-content-marketing

https://www.niams.nih.gov/health_info/Acne/acne_ff.asp

https://blog.kissmetrics.com/social-media-for-b2b/

https://www.oktopost.com/blog/b2b-inbound-marketing/

http://www.marketing-schools.org/types-of-marketing/b2b-marketing.html

http://study.com/academy/lesson/what-is-b2b-marketing-definition-examples-quiz.html

https://blog.hubspot.com/marketing/content-marketing-plan

https://www.b2bmarketing.net/en-gb/resources/blog/5-benefits-b2b-content-marketing-your-business

http://www.business2community.com/b2b-marketing/7-benefits-b2b-marketing-plan-01425351#RcEcD5yDUUV2mxtm.97

http://www.streetdirectory.com/travel_guide/193138/marketing/new_benefits_in_b2b_marketing.html

https://www.becomingminimalist.com/15-reasons-i-think-you-should-blog/

http://www.socialmediaexaminer.com/attract-more-blog-readers/

https://business.tutsplus.com/tutorials/create-and-host-a-webinar-for-free-using-google-hangouts--cms-21805

https://blog.hubspot.com/marketing/examples-of-user-generated-content

http://www.curata.com/blog/content-marketing-user-generated-content/

https://blog.hubspot.com/marketing/content-marketing-plan

http://www.writersdigest.com/online-editor/the-12-dos-and-donts-of-writing-a-blog

https://letterpile.com/writing/Ten-Tips-On-Writing-And-Publishing-Hubs-At-Hubpages-And-Making-Money

http://www.mequoda.com/articles/digital-magazine-publishing/digital-publishing-tips-and-strategies/

http://www.bizible.com/blog/how-your-b2b-marketing-funnel-works

http://elitedaily.com/life/why-id-rather-watch-shows-than-go-out/1357111

http://www.willatworklearning.com/2006/05/people_remember.html

http://www.mequoda.com/articles/digital-magazine-publishing/digital-publishing-tips-and-strategies/

https://www.americanexpress.com/us/small-business/openforum/articles/7-tips-to-win-any-negotiation/

http://time.com/3007520/be-more-powerful/

http://time.com/3007520/be-more-powerful/

http://www.businessinsider.com/how-to-become-more-powerful-2011-12?op=1/#lp-powerful-people-feel-good-about-themselves-4

http://www.rasmussen.edu/degrees/business/blog/industry-insights-before-starting-marketing-career/

http://diymusician.cdbaby.com/music-promotion/top-5-things-you-need-to-have-before-you-start-marketing-your-music/

https://localfirstbank.com/article/5-things-you-need-before-you-start-marketing-your-small-business/

https://www.inc.com/guides/2010/08/10-things-to-do-before-you-start-your-start-up.html

https://www.scu.edu/mobi/business-courses/starting-a-business/session-13-opening-and-marketing/

https://bench.co/syllabus/bookkeeping/separate-business-personal-finances/

www.ingramcontent.com/pod-product-compliance
Lightning Source LLC
Chambersburg PA
CBHW070924220526
45470CB00012B/1671